DEMCO

Art Smart

How to Draw Cartoons

Christine Smith

For a free color catalog describing Gareth Stevens Publishing's list of high-quality books and multimedia programs, call 1-800-542-2595 (USA) or 1-800-461-9120 (Canada). Gareth Stevens Publishing's Fax: (414) 225-0377. See our catalog, too, on the World Wide Web: http://gsinc.com

Library of Congress Cataloging-in-Publication Data available upon request from the publisher. Fax: (414) 225-0377 for the attention of the Publishing Records Department.

ISBN 0-8368-1709-5

First published in North America in 1997 by
Gareth Stevens Publishing
1555 North RiverCenter Drive, Suite 201
Milwaukee, Wisconsin, 53212, USA

Original © 1996 by Regency House Publishing Limited (Troddy Books imprint), The Grange, Grange Yard, London, England, SE1 3AG. Text and illustrations by Christine Smith. Additional end matter © 1997 by Gareth Stevens, Inc.

Printed in the United States of America

1 2 3 4 5 6 7 8 9 0 1 00 99 98 97

Gareth Stevens Publishing
MILWAUKEE

Materials

Drawing pencils have letters printed on them to show the firmness of the lead. Pencils with an *H* have very hard lead. Pencils with an *HB* have medium lead. Pencils with a *B* have soft lead. Use an *HB* pencil to draw the outlines in this book. Then use a *B* pencil to complete the drawings.

This type of pencil sharpener works well because it keeps the shavings inside a container.

Once you have drawn the outlines on a piece of paper, place a thinner sheet of paper over them. Then make a clean, finished drawing, leaving out any unnecessary lines.

Use a soft eraser to make any changes you might want. Color your drawings with felt-tip pens, watercolors, crayons, or colored pencils.

Shapes

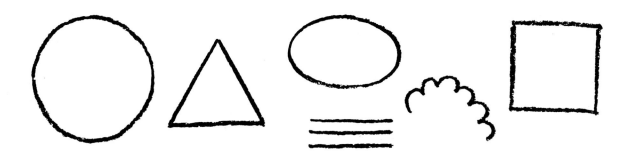

Before you begin drawing, practice the shapes above. Draw them over and over again. All the drawings in this book are based on these simple shapes.

Color

Mixing colors is fun whether you are using colored pencils or paints. Mix red and yellow to make orange. Mix blue and yellow to make green. Red and blue make purple.

The key to making good cartoons
is to start mainly with circles,
squares, and other simple shapes.
Cartoon faces can be drawn
by using circles like this.

Drawings are funnier if you use
a mixture of shapes — thick
upper bodies with thin legs,
little bodies with big heads, big
noses on little faces, short
bodies with long legs,
long bodies with
short legs, and so on.
Have fun drawing
all sorts of shapes!

Happy

Sad

Angry

Shy

Scared

Ill

Puzzled

Crying

Laughing

MORE IDEAS
Try all kinds of ways to draw the eyes, nose,
and mouth to make different expressions.
To get ideas, look in the mirror and make faces!

Funny faces

1 Walking	**2**	**3**	**4**
1 Running	**2**	**3**	**4**
1 Jumping	**2**	**3**	**4**
Start with the head and upper body.	Draw action into the arms.	Add the legs in this position.	Add speed and movement lines. Finish with details.

Action figures

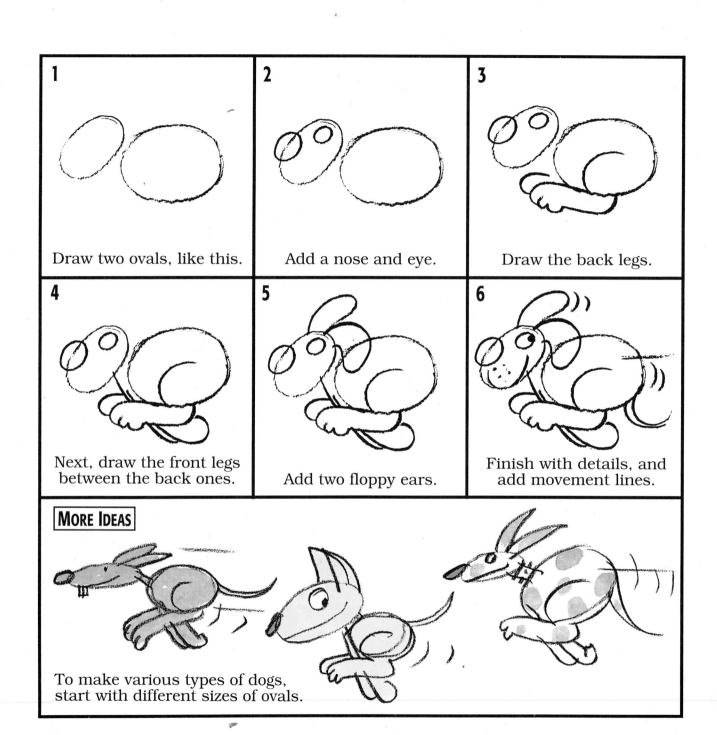

1 Draw two ovals, like this.

2 Add a nose and eye.

3 Draw the back legs.

4 Next, draw the front legs between the back ones.

5 Add two floppy ears.

6 Finish with details, and add movement lines.

MORE IDEAS

To make various types of dogs, start with different sizes of ovals.

Dashing dog

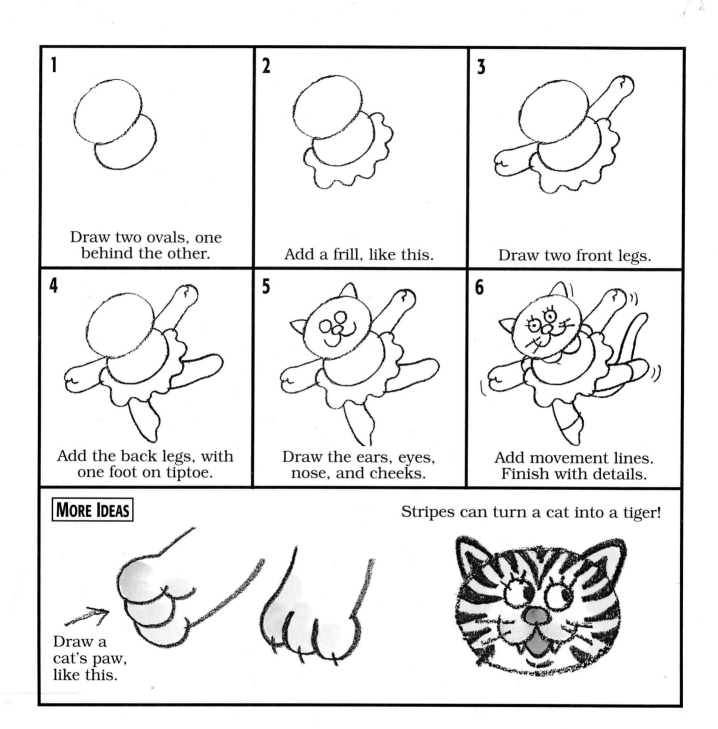

1 Draw two ovals, one behind the other.

2 Add a frill, like this.

3 Draw two front legs.

4 Add the back legs, with one foot on tiptoe.

5 Draw the ears, eyes, nose, and cheeks.

6 Add movement lines. Finish with details.

MORE IDEAS

Stripes can turn a cat into a tiger!

Draw a cat's paw, like this.

12

Dancing cat

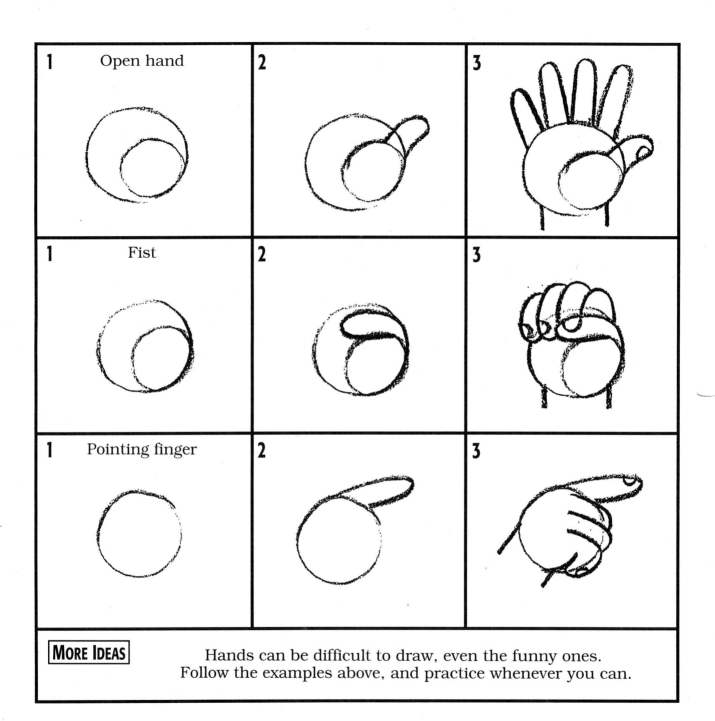

1 Open hand	2	3
1 Fist	2	3
1 Pointing finger	2	3

MORE IDEAS

Hands can be difficult to draw, even the funny ones.
Follow the examples above, and practice whenever you can.

Helpful hands

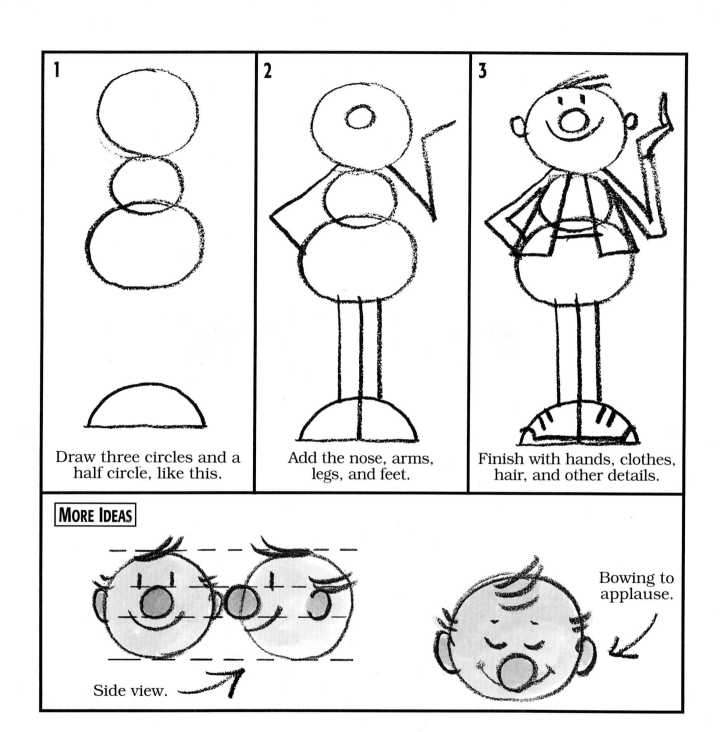

1

Draw three circles and a half circle, like this.

2

Add the nose, arms, legs, and feet.

3

Finish with hands, clothes, hair, and other details.

MORE IDEAS

Side view.

Bowing to applause.

The comedian

1 Draw a large circle.

2 Add a spout and a handle.

3 Draw a lid and a base.

4 Add a round eye and a curved mouth.

5 Draw a hand and legs, like this.

6 Add details of curly hair, eyelashes, and shoes.

MORE IDEAS

Draw faces, arms, and legs on other household shapes.

Tessa Teapot

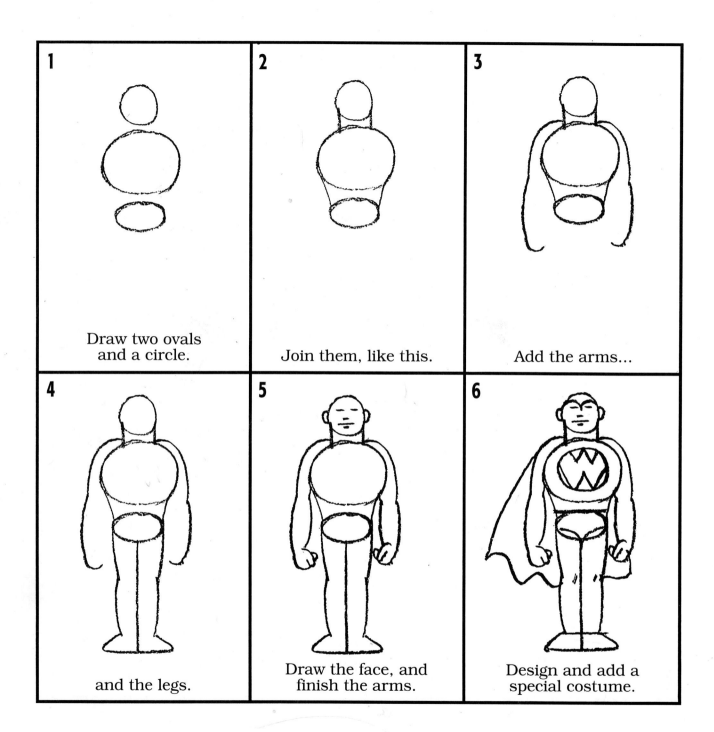

1 Draw two ovals and a circle.

2 Join them, like this.

3 Add the arms...

4 and the legs.

5 Draw the face, and finish the arms.

6 Design and add a special costume.

Wonderman

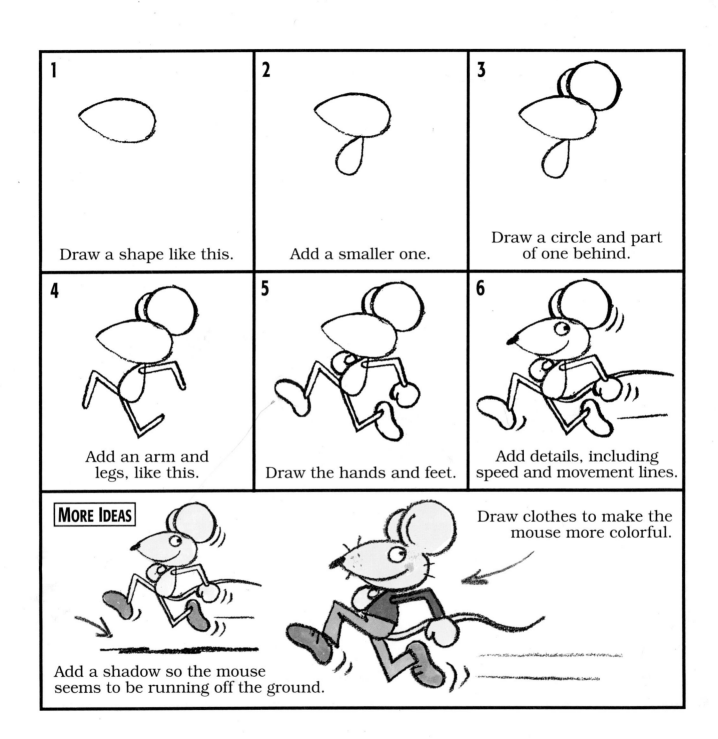

1

Draw a shape like this.

2

Add a smaller one.

3

Draw a circle and part of one behind.

4

Add an arm and legs, like this.

5

Draw the hands and feet.

6

Add details, including speed and movement lines.

MORE IDEAS

Draw clothes to make the mouse more colorful.

Add a shadow so the mouse seems to be running off the ground.

Running mouse

More Books to Read

Cartoon Fun. Hal Tollison (W. Foster Publishing)
Cartooning for Kids. Carol Benjamin (HarperCollins Children's Books)
Cartooning for Young Children. Vic Lockman (V. Lockman)
Draw, Model, and Paint (series). (Gareth Stevens)
Drawing Cartoons. Judy Tatchell (EDC)
Drawing Funny Faces. Watermill Press Staff (Troll Communications)
How to Draw Cartoons and Caricatures. J. Tatchell (EDC)
I Can Draw Cartoon Animals. (W. Foster Publishing)
Worldwide Crafts (series). Deshpande/MacLeod-Brudenell (Gareth Stevens)

Videos

Animation for Kids. (Bullfrog Films)
Cartoon Forms. (Roland Collection)
Cartoon People. (Agency for Instructional Technology)
Funny Faces. (Agency for Instructional Technology)

Web Sites

http://www.go-interface.com/fridgeartz
http://finalfront.com/kids/art/art.htm

Index

action figures 8-9

cat 12-13
colored pencils 2, 3
colors 3
comedian 16-17
crayons 2

dog 10-11
drawing pencils 2

eraser 2

expressions 6-7

faces, funny 4, 6-7
felt-tip pens 2

hands 14-15

mouse 22-23
movement lines 8, 10, 12, 22

paints 3

pencil sharpener 2

shapes 3, 4
speed lines 8, 22

teapot 18-19
tiger 12

watercolors 2
Wonderman 20-21